The Texture of Days, in Ash and Leaf

The Texture of Days,
in Ash and Leaf

Bruce Kauffman

First Edition

Hidden Brook Press
www.HiddenBrookPress.com
writers@HiddenBrookPress.com

Copyright © 2013 Hidden Brook Press
Copyright © 2013 Bruce Kauffman

All rights for poems revert to the author. All rights for book, layout and design remain with Hidden Brook Press. No part of this book may be reproduced except by a reviewer who may quote brief passages in a review. The use of any part of this publication reproduced, transmitted in any form or by any means, electronic, mechanical, photocopied, recorded or otherwise stored in a retrieval system without prior written consent of the publisher is an infringement of the copyright law.

The Texture of Days, in Ash and Leaf
by Bruce Kauffman

Editor – Carolyn Smart
Cover Photograph – Eleanor Leonne Bennett
Cover Design – Richard M. Grove
Layout and Design – Richard M. Grove

Typeset in Arial

Printed and bound in USA

Library and Archives Canada Cataloguing in Publication

Kauffman, Bruce, 1950-
    The texture of days, in ash and leaf / Bruce Kauffman.

(North Shore series)
Poems.
ISBN 978-1-897475-86-7

    I. Title. II. Series: North Shore series.

PS8621.A685T49 2012   C811'.6   C2012-906439-4

Acknowledgements

I would like to offer a very sincere thank you to Carolyn Smart for her incredibly helpful advice, compassionate eye and gentle hand while editing my first full collection of poetry.

I would also like to offer an equally special thank you to Catherine Owen, Sandra Ridley, Jason Heroux and Jeanette Lynes for taking the time to read this as a manuscript, and then offer their comments for inclusion on the back cover. Thank you all, as well, for your personal remarks.

I would like to offer a very deep thank you to Eleanor Leonne Bennett for sharing a piece of her brilliant collection for the cover artwork of this book.

I'd like to extend a generous thanks to my publisher, Richard Grove - Tai, for his encouragement and to Hidden Brook Press for seeing a possibility in this work.

I would also like to offer a "back in the day" distant, but very real, thank you to Catherine O'Neil Thorn and to all of those there connected with the "Toads in the Garden" reading series who helped me believe in both poetry and myself as a poet in that time and in that light.

I would also like to extend an ongoing and heartfelt thank you to the ever-growing family of poets, authors and guests at the poetry @ the artel open mic reading series for your support, your encouragement – your voices always giving the words on the page a beating heart.

And a very deeply felt thank you to all in my life you have either encouraged or inspired. There simply are not enough pages to list. I would like each of you to know that even as innocently as it was given, as innocuous as it seemed – it was noticed. And it is neither lost nor forgotten.

Table of Contents

Acknowledgements – *p. vii*

Preface – *p. 1*

Places – *p. 2*
roots – *p. 4*
hunger – *p. 5*
well meant – *p. 7*
5am, in mourning – *p. 8*
stones – *p. 11*
light, eulogy – *p. 12*
society – *p. 19*
pages – *p. 20*
wonder – *p. 21*
review – *p. 23*
crossing – *p. 26*
unsure – *p. 27*
copper highways – *p. 28*
copper highways, slight return – *p. 31*
a conclusion – *p. 35*
deliverance – *p. 36*
spirit ii – *p. 37*
for my father – *p. 39*
sight – *p. 47*
the edge – *p. 49*
holding – *p. 54*
city limits – *p. 55*
still water – *p. 58*
doors – *p. 64*

birthright – *p. 66*
perpetuity – *p. 71*
from a precipice – *p. 73*
cancer – *p. 79*
prisoner – *p. 81*
weight – *p. 83*
mirror – *p. 88*
barrio – *p. 89*
rain – *p. 93*
tribute – *p. 95*
passage – *p. 102*
shadows – *p. 105*
language – *p. 108*
destiny – *p. 112*
reading – *p. 113*
today – *p. 117*
seed – *p. 119*
shade and shadow – *p. 120*
legends – *p. 121*
death – *p. 123*
spirit – *p. 126*
void – *p. 128*
solitude – *p. 131*

Author Biographical Note – *p. 135*

Cover artist's Bio – *p. 137*

*I want to tell what the forests
were like*

*I will have to speak
in a forgotten language*

*W.S. Merwin,
"Witness" from "The Rain in the Trees"
Knopf Press, 1988*

PREFACE

This collection of poems, small handfuls of water dipped from an ocean of word, were written between the years of 1994 to 1997 – a time in my life believing that nothing was and then understanding that everything is. A time of endings. A time of beginnings. A time of stumbling, sorting through the rubble and the flowers of each.

It was also a time, after years of neglect – of having set both book and pen aside, this then a passionate re-emergence into the written word. There is an old Sioux saying – "The longest journey you will ever make is from your head to your heart." This period of time in my life, for me, was both that realization – and then actualization.

It was, as well, a period of poetic discovery – from a time of taking my own ideas of managed and corralled poetry to another place. This discovery of layers of silence above emptiness. I've heard the soundless whispers there – these words arriving, connected, in trails of themselves – and in those times, I but the translator, the interpreter, the conduit, the pen. These words coming from nowhere that I know – flowing onto an always waiting and blank page.

Bruce Kauffman

places

take me to those places
I should never leave
to that colour in the forest
to that palace never built

      that vision made
      of glass and dream
      pieces of rock and shadow
      where the palace rests
          but is never seen

take me to that dream
that waits for a vision
waits for an eye
waits for a mind

      then waits for an
      empty space
      in the back
          of that mind

take me to the spaces
between the thoughts
between the words
      where wonder lies
      where the water waits

      where the universe
         sleeps
      where the future
         lives

take me to the depth
of the night
      where all things
      become as they are

      without mask
      without face

      without an eye
      to the passage
           of time

take me to the home
of the poet

to that home on the path
from a thousand graves

allow me time
to touch the names
     carved in the markers

let me feel
the warmth of
     the earth
inhale the lilac
     and thyme

and watch the evening
weep at dusk
through a hole
in the sun

in tears that wash
all colour and light
     from the sky

         then

take me
to the place

     the colour
        goes

roots

this
      these

ties
      that nourish
      and feed
      and strengthen

           and grow

           and provide

           and protect and

                  imprison

hunger

who am I
to speak of hunger

when even the sound
of the word
      in my own mouth
           seems full

when my own mouth
has only gargled
in the sour taste of
    complication
    obstruction
    hesitation and
        all forgotten
            as I spit them out…

        but

how hard for you
when hunger is
your only meal

for you
how hard
to expel desolation's
    aftertaste

to wash out
that bitter swill

    of isolation

how difficult
to rinse that gagging
metallic film of

   helplessness
   that coats
     your tongue
     your throat
     your mind

     your heart

that gnawing pain
relieving itself
only in bloat
   then lethargy

   then hopelessness

     as the road that
     was laid before you
       dims and fades
         against your back

   and

as you look up
into the slowly
   blurring vision
     of your mother's face
you understand
   that there is
     but one
       question

and as you close
your eyes

   the world swallows
     another answer

well meant

i am

resolutions
good intentions
plans of action
decisions and

the single
      biggest exception
      to nearly all of my rules

5am, in mourning

too many poets passing
      leaving
on thin icy sheets
on sheets white and
      soiled

was the thread so thin
      this fine thread of words
which bound us together
that we break and we
fray
      so easily
      so quietly

for whom do we weep as
the beauty unravels
thread by thread and the
spirit is bared in
      naked confession and
      guiltless exposure

this pen
my pen lies
      still
      on a blood-stained
          table
the endless reminder
      of time

times when i've stabbed
      and plunged
          and drug
its crimson tip through
the deepest most place
in my heart

                lest i forget to feel
                how it used to feel
                how i need to feel
                         how i need it to feel

this pen
my pen lies
         still

and always

it, the line
and the point
         in its grip
         in its texture
                  in its passion

that point that defined
the inward
         from all other

and again
this morning
         that distinction
         falls down into
                  thin shades of grey

and the lines fall apart
as my skin stretches taut
over another empty
injustice

```
        my fingers, calloused
        my head is weary
              my heart is empty
              pounding the blood of the
                    heartless through the
                          veins of the world


  still here, restless
  i lie awake
        in this twilight
  as the haze of the dew
  remains in my eye
        i see some semblance
        of my pen
              bloody, useless
                    and wicked
  it lies on my table

  i reach for its touch

                    its ink
                          my morphine

                    its mistress
                          my life
```

stones

i sat
silently
and watched
them laying the
stones of the path
for the eldest daughter

and the fear in her eye

as for an instant
      and for the first time

      she saw them too

light, eulogy
for William Stafford

*...If a different call came there wouldn't be any
world, or you, or the river, or the owls calling.*

*How you stand here is important. How you
listen for the next things to happen. How you breathe.*
William Stafford: from "Being a Person"

i.

i'm sorry
i didn't know

i'd never heard

someone should have
told me

and i'm sorry

i'm sorry

i'm sorry

      i didn't know

but today i find
you'd stolen
a good part
of the light

and now i know

that when i opened
my eyes this morning
to what they
called light

and i
defined as day

i was deceived

deceived
by what i know now

is shadow

i didn't know

i didn't know

you

you

you'd looked
down the path
this same path
i watch today

and there
here
you'd reached
with your pen
and you'd taken
    a piece of light
        from the sky

and you didn't know

you didn't mean
    to hold it

you meant to
    set it free

but they say
you had a splinter
of it left in your
half-closed eye

and a soft piece of light
gently clenched
    in your cold soft palm

    as they
went with their spades
to carve a piece
of dirt into
grave

ii.

they say
that in perfect light

you can see
all the way
      around the world

horizon does not
hold back sight

but instead
only holds up
our own
      blue shadow

horizon rests
as unsettled breeze
and carries back leaves

this restless swirling
around these autumn trees

these trees
of wonder
      half spent

in this wood
of half forgotten
      sound

iii.

i was drawn
from the darkness
by this distant
multicoloured forest
      of mirror
      and glass

and it was here
in this grey light

but soft light
      nonetheless

here where
the shadows ran long
and grew and grew

along the ground
until each shadow
became not itself
but each instead
as well the one beside

and my sliding sun
slowly slipping below
an edge of earth and sky

and leaving behind
this slowly widening
broadening
deepening darkness

these shadowy
floating dark ghosts
swallowing any piece
      upon where each
           colour was

and it is here

it is now

it is through a distant
memory's ears

here
from these empty spaces
in the darkness

here
where the rays
of the sun used to glide

here
that i hear
these crystalline echoes
      of empty hearts
      calling

these hearts

      like prisms

      in the darkness

and these hearts
now in the tongue
of tomorrow's light

and forever
whispering
      to the sun

society

with crutch in hand
        we ride the backside
                of the cutting edge

and we
ever cautious
ever so vigilant
stand and
        lean into
        the winds of change

as we forever fly
the tattered
and soiled
        flag of tradition and

it was but an hour ago
that they
stood
there
        anxious
        and fearful

as they watched
and they wept
        as we
        left the cave

pages

and i reached
in this book
for the piece
of a page
on which you
wrote your note

and to the touch
the slick and
glossy paper
felt porous
and rough

the ink against
my finger
only cold

i rubbed the words
until
my fingers bled

the blood
staining the page
into the colours
of the setting sun

wonder

i touched the walls
of the parthenon
when i was a child
and it was new

i measured the weight
of the blocks of stone
as we built the third pyramid
until the transports came

       and i counted
       the dead

i sat on one end
of the great wall
of china
and watched it slither
and wind motionless

       as the other end
       was tied with
       a string to the moon

and i was the eye
of a bird as i looked down
on a desert floor
and caught an image of the sun
in an empty mirage

       until it became the edge
       of darkness stealing my own
       shadow turned into night

and in different flesh
these bones have skated
on all the glass
even before the canyons
and ravines defined themselves
and became but pathway to the
onslaught of heat and ice

and i
touched
wonder
      before there was

      wonder

but i
never realized
how little i'd seen

how helpless i was

until i
reached
with my thumb
      to wipe a tear

           from your eye

review
for C. O.

and she said
take the eraser
to every page
    you've ever
    known
        or thought

close your eyes
then disown
    their sockets

discard logic
then your
    senses

forget time

then your body

then your name

wait
for the blanket
    of silence
    and slide into it

    then discover
        your arms

    and slowly reach
        with open hands
        uplifted palms

    and find in one
        an eye

   in the other
      a heart

assume nothing

deny nothing

then rediscover
a face
   forgotten

and put this
new face on

   one side
   singed by
      the lapping flames
      of a raging fire

   and the other
   brushed in
      the icy blush
      of freshly fallen snow

and only then
open your eyes
   to the first
      image there

        and

against a canvas
    of humility

with one finger
dipped in tears
    trace the outline
        of that image

        and

with another finger
dipped in blood
    colour in
        its shadow

        then

step back
    to watch it

    fade

    or breathe

crossing

whenever you are asked

to be but one
      or the other

asked

to be but the river
      or the bridge

become neither

become both

      become the water

unsure

am i the reincarnation
of some lost poet
      or just the incineration
      of yesterday's news

am i the resurrection
of some lost friendship
      or just some friend lost
      without rescue in the wood

is my fate inspired
by the ebbing tide in lunar motion
      or merely in quiet conspiracy
      of a lunatic's hand and flowing notion

is my destiny set in play
by the colours fixed in fate
or must i blindly swing
my cane of emotion
      upon the latch
      of freedom's gate

copper highways

I think that I've been here before.
They call it "deja vu".
But, no, this feels like something real.

Naw, I'm beginning to think that I
haven't been here before.

This is ridiculous.
I know that I've never been here before.

I was born long after they closed this place down.

I was born in . . . . . .

i see copper vats
i see the cauldrons

i see the kettles being
 formed

i am a child

my father mined the ore
near the russian town of kirov
my mother played
the balalaika

my father mined the fields
in the great depression
i watched the cotton turn
to ash and watched the cattle die

my mother gave me up for
dead when i didn't come home
from what was and wasn't
the war to end all wars

i stood on the threshold of
the twentieth century wondering
realizing i would
never witness the twenty first

i was a loyalist
but branded a traitor
as i left in haste
one night heading north
      and never looked back

i stood on the shore of
every land and watched
an intruder discover and
claim my home land

my father taught me
to hunt the bison when
the berries froze -
i pray for their souls

      the bison
      the berries
      my father's
      my own

i have visions
fleeting
of ice and then of
stone and flint

    i clearly see
           the first sunrise
           the last sunset

i hold memories
vague
of another world
another place

        warm
        secure
        euphoric

we are descendants
all
        of a single atom
        a single force
        a single moment
        a single thought
        a common passion

histories shared
        i am a part of you
        as much as each of you
        a part of me........................

But this is impossible

I was born in.........

.....and you see i still
        refuse to admit
        what we should have
        already known

copper highways, slight return

i have atoned for my sins
but haven't learned

my past clings to me
      hauntingly unfamiliar
visions fly like
      forbidden passion

        am i alone
        the gatekeeper
        to tomorrow
        or are the voices
        i hear in the foreground
        comrades in
        deception

i am a part of
every creature come
gone and every
being yet to live

i have smelled the
danger in the laughter
and tasted the anger
in the silence

i've stood in awe and
watched effortless change
and helplessly stood alone
weeping at endless coercion

i've seen the sparrow fly
and men fall
in disgrace

i've experienced the futility
of speaking to a man of war
about the beauty of
the setting sun
and realized how foolish
to disturb this evening's
colour with thoughts about
the inevitability of war

i've seen death in disaster
and a friend die an
arm's length away and

in either case could do
nothing

i've seen love blossom
i've watched love die

i've seen senseless hatred
and paralysing fear

i've witnessed the passion
in a lover's eye
and the poison in
the critic's pen

i've watched as compassion
measured in ounces fill
an emptiness measured
in tonnes

i've seen them hide
in the darkness and
laugh in the daylight
yet failed to hear
what they were thinking

i've seen everything

i've seen nothing

i've learned everything
and nothing at all

i am darkness in
the midday sun
and but a candle to
the night sky

my past has no
beginning

my future has
no end

i will be here
for eternity

i shall be here
but an instant

i am the home for
wisdom waiting
for a home - both
watching waiting

i am lucky
to be alive
    to be lucky
      to be alive....................

        but i was born
        in a month

        beneath the same crescent
        moon i watch this evening

        crescent moon
        silhouette
            behind the clouds

        disappears

a conclusion

expectation

a pit with no
bottom

and always
and only
a feather
waiting
      for a wing

         on a camel's
            back

deliverance

i've become so inhibited
that this pen burns my fingers

it has become
        foreign
        alien
        a stranger

and i've become
suspended in a box
with each side
but an arm and a half
or a leg and a half's
        length away

suffocation comes
now

in streams
        of colour
and degrees
        of shade
stolen from all
of the flowers

        in an ever
        shrinking
        summer

spirit ii

why only this package
of bones and flesh
with which to enshroud
a spirit inside
        the size of tomorrow

is this skin
        so elastic
the spirit
        compressed

and how to now measure
these bits of compassion

and how to calibrate
these hints of concern

how many chances
will these eyes be given
to perceive the beauty

how many hearts
within me
beat
        in love
        in lust
                in pain

tell me

is there
but one answer
that transcends
all, every question

and is that answer but
a single word

and then is that word
but a single letter

and has that letter
but a single sound

and is that sound
not heard

but thought

and is that thought
instead but a vision
humbled by the darkness
of the evening

and lost in the shadow
of another night

lost again on the bridge
to the edge of the morning only

to find itself

        again

once more
sitting lightly
    on the unmade
        bed of horizon and

calmly resting
as it waits
    for itself in
        tomorrow's sigh

for my father

i.

i never cried at
my father's funeral.
i sat in the pew
at the foot of the altar

i wasn't there

i was lost in the
memory of an
open eye

ii.

for him
for nearly a decade
for one seventh
a life
for every monday
or wednesday
or saturday
lost

confined inside
these four walls
where the mind
remained
even when it
was away

the world to
which it
knew it must
return

and every day
a step further
removed
from the life
that was
assumed would
      always be

every day
a step removed
toward a life
become
becoming

                ever beneath
                the tepid
                tranquil water
                lies a thunderous
                cold and
                crashing wave

his
a world condensed
from the earth and sky

to these shrinking walls

to this stagnant air

to the monotonous
repetitive forgotten talk

to the agony of never
knowing

to a shivering fear
concealed

to the smothering
dependence

and to the disdain
for that blanket of
pity and hopeless regret

until and finally
an instant of
      uncertain euphoria
then lightening

then
  nothing

nothing
  anymore of
  this world

iii.

a chair waits empty
for the spirit
that warmed it

waits empty
beside a globe
a postcard and
a magnifying lens

        echoes that became
        new worlds for slowly
        failing eyes
        and unguided
        anarchic limbs

and a comb waits without
a head to brush

and a cane sits without
a hand to hold

and a shadow sleeps without
a light
        to make it strong

        or real

beside that chair
my father's
bible, globe
and looking glass

all the places
he could no longer go

    and now his only
      ticket there

iv.

and there were no
words

there was no time

no place
to say "goodbye"

no words to say
"i love you"

no words
no time
no place

no need

      the message
      ever clear

and i stand here
with no answer
but faith
as i stand beside
my endless
questions

      these ageless questions
      of forever child

V.

and no one saw
me cry at my
father's funeral

but not even one of us could explain
why the mist that fell
from the sky that morning
was as warm as blood
and left small streams
of wet salt
        on our cheeks

                in our eyes

sight

we weep for
the motherless fawn

through shades
    of ethiopia
through the haze
    of bangladesh

    the children are
        dying

we curse this trail
of relentless war

through the blinds
    of bosnia
through the shadow
    of iraq
through the walls
    of iran
through the iron
    curtain parted

through the windswept sand
on the city streets
of the world

    the children are
        dying

we share our passions
share our words

through lips parted
through lips closed
through lips joined

        together
through lips lost
      in thought

through lips waiting
      to be joined

      to be silent

through lips cracked
      in smile

lips cracked by
      the sun

cracked in
      the icy air

cracked

      by a blow
      from the back
      of a hand

and

through the keyholes
of doors frozen
with hinges rusted
in tears
newly shed

      the children are

          watching

the edge

you speak fluently of roses
I understand nothing of flowers

I tell of the sweet smell of
the earth tilled in early morning
you are of the sky

I am the morning, blue
you are the grey at dusk

        they watch, they believe they know
        they think they see
        yet they cannot catch without shaded eye
        the passionate eclipse —

                first came the fear
                yet in the fear, the beauty
                      that beauty lost, now,
                      to wisdom
                and children watch with covered eye

in the end it seemed so clear

    there is no truth in clarity

we were shells upon the beach, shining
discovered - found, then displayed
upon mantels over raging fires
        lost now beneath old sheets and shirts
        in a cardboard box - we brittle, stale
        laid to rest in a cellar grave or musty attic

        above, below - arbitrary, surely
        seashells have no sin

I was so sure I understood

    there is no truth in understanding

I believed passion to be elusive

soft - like satin, and satin-like
easy to fall away

I discovered in love's flight

      her temperament and in that
      temperament, her freedom
          and in that freedom - the wonder

I was, I am, certain that in this
life I shared your destiny
today, I realize, as much as I should
I could but barely touch your pain
pain like a river -
    like a river ever-flowing

    but in that river, still, together
    we saw our faces reflected

what must the river give
to become part, the ocean

    there is no truth in isolation

I wanted truth to be radiant -
        to ride in on a white stallion
        in hand, her silver sword glinting high
        her hair flowing, cape gently blowing
        and I could look straight into her shining eyes

        there is no stallion

I found truth instead in gutters -
        sleeping, dishevelled clumps of
        dirty flesh and clothes, without
        a home, in gutter stench -
        nearly dead
                yet not
        alive - barely
                lifeless eyes - on the edge
                life, death - on the edge
                      alive, a spark -
                              in desolation struck
                              along the edge of hope

it is on the edge we

always stand -
        on the edge
                what was
                what will

    edge to edge

    edge on edge
           on edge on edge

    cliff top

           valley

between
        between
until
in the end
        that final valley
        lost and

                gives rise again, another time
                another time,
                      a newer voice
                            as
we the ancestors
        then become

and there

there on an edge where
attics, cellars have no measure
        to a child
attics, cellars of no value
        to a child -
            but boxes
            only boxes

and in the bottom of a box
of yellow, faded, musty
sheets and shirts -

    with tiny hands, sea shells tossed
    gently back into the sea……….

……. somewhere in the distance, I
  can hear the children's laughter

holding

i hold a faded
portrait
of the past
      with edges
         sharp as razors

this picture
of broken glass

and of the words
      we no longer
         speak

city limits

this evening, you're as
quiet as i've ever seen you

you're like a monday
morning at four o'clock

i can almost relate

i peer down your streets
soft water-colour
charcoal grey

      lights and lines
      defining what is

but you are only city
you are not truth

and lights and lines
only pretend
      to know as much
as the leaf aimlessly teetering
restlessly across the park

streets maps only begin
to tell as much as
the broken wine bottle
      lost beside your curb

your city truth only ends
when we forget
      to tow the line

                stumble across that fine line
                        razor sharp razor thin
              glistening
                cutting

last night i slit all
my wrists with a razor-
edged truth

        they refused to bleed
        i refused to die but
                i can still smell the sweet stench
                of the blood red stains on the walls

                inside my head

crimson reminders
of the truths

        past

lessons
painfully found
        then lost
        then found
                then forgotten

we yearned for truth

we paid for truth
with small change and
proved we didn't understand
        how little we knew

        how little we cared
to remember until

      we forgot them both

           the truth
           the cost

                but we were young
                we were immortal
                we revelled in that freedom
                      got lost inside that freedom
                lost

like tonight
on a dark city alley

lost inside the city
locked outside of truth

                real truth has no
                home in the city except

                for an instant
                    before dawn
                as the city sleeps and
                the dead open their eyes
                    and sing yesterday's
                  songs
                        to the sunrise

still water

i.

i stood alone
behind a thousand visions
      unfolding just ahead

i felt the presence
of a thousand mornings
      here in one
as the washed ghosts
of a hundred people
      came into view

i watched the milk
coloured clouds part
the blue of the sky

      and nothing filled the void

i watched
as the spirits
ancient
walked the wood
in the naked hours
      of the leanest light

the morning dew
remaining on the leaves
proved to me
that the night-time
did weep

      for the sunrise

and i looked
into the rising sun
      felt no warmth
      saw no light

but on the horizon
saw a single
      red thread of hope

i've tried to measure
the distance between
thought
      and love
trickery
      and magic

the notes in a chord

the world we understand
      and the one in which we live

and the distance between each
now
always
the distance from
      the moon
      to the sun

ii.

i watched as the flowers
in the window box
      burgundy
      yellow
      violet

          moist

understood the rain
far better than i

and will welcome the frost
more easily
than i can
      accept my own

i try to learn
i try to teach

but what am i
who am i
to teach

a million mornings
anything

when the sunrise
ten thousand years ago
understood even then

that thought
was distraction

that warmth and love
can neither be taught
          nor explained

that the arc of the sun was
really the second illusion

that man became blind
not by looking into the sun
but instead by looking away

and that shadow is not
          the absence of light but
                    instead the consumption of it

iii.

surely the first man
in that first cave
understood his universe
      far better than i

but i remain

and i have seen
that the dead can't die
when i've stood on a mountain peak
and felt a dead friend's words
      slip into my spirit
and another's passion flow
      through the tip of my pen

i begin to realize
that the tears
that hurt the most

      change the most

and are in the end
but shadow
and rain

and i
darkened
wet
remain
still

here in this place

here in these times
where sometimes

there is an ocean
between laughter
and joy

a river
between friendship
      and stranger

and but a teardrop
between the past
      and the future

doors

boxes of half
finished poems
fill the room
with the same
    cautious celebration

as birthday balloons
    in a nursing home

and in the darkest
    part of the room
vision wanders
    loses its focus
        then
    loses its source

eyes open
    blinking
    searching

for doors
    to open
    to close
    to enter

        to escape

and in another life
i lived in a world
    without doors

where thresholds
    were slides

and in a place
without doors

and nothing
      to protect
      from nothing
           to hide

in that world
without boundary

without direction

where the dead
discard the weight
      of their useless
           corpses

and soar
      as memories

           of memory
               waiting

birthright

and for only an instant
you at birth - each of us
    the nation-less
    colourless
    genderless child

and for but that same instant
the world was a door
    held
      wide open

and your only tie
to its threshold

    instinctual

as your heart
    had even the voice

the will to push
    you forward
    to suckle
    to breathe

but not so high overhead
the winds of knowledge
gently blow to swing doors shut

into perceptual locks
and societal latches
all long forged
    in history's mill

and in that, this mixture
of gentle breeze and wicked wind

of times before

and before

and before

and before

and before there were prisons
there were barely visible
cold steel bars

and long before thought
there were eyes
closed shut

and before there were eyes
there were walls
waiting

      to be seen

and it is here
was there
in only that instant
your instant at birth

      you remember

everything

the walls

the eyes
open
        then shut

and you hear
all the words
that ever were

in all the tongues
in all the forms

and in that instant
that single instant
in all the sounds
and flashes of light

        everything that ever was
           passes through

and then in the ensuing instant
of silence

        you watch

        you hear

everything

that is

        as yet to come

       yet to be

and you become

        omniscient breath

in a gasp

    for air
    and life

omniscient breath
calling back
    to wisdom's wind

as you climb
the walls

breathe through
    their cracks
see through
    the emptiness
which thrust them
    up right through
    their shadows

and you wear
the face
of every child
    ever been
    ever coming

and they cut
your resurrection
    cord

and they name
you "hope"

and they give
you tomorrow

and they wash your eyes
with a cotton swabbed haze
swirled from their
      own bottle of memory

then they take you
from your mother
and wrap you in a blanket
of woven gender and race
      spun on ancient looms
           no one now understands

and in all of your life
in all of your time that remains

in those flecks of
thread
wind
and time passing

in those instants
in only those instants

      outside of thought
      outside of time

are left the fingerprints
of your reaching to touch

all the things
      we'd ever lost

and prints left now

upon all the things
      we're losing

perpetuity

the perpetual motion
of the shuffle of generations

footsteps falling
into heart steps
    waiting

each falling
    effortlessly
    aimlessly
    down then up

this multi-directional
stairway

each footstep always
the first one forward

    and in the shadow
    the next one back

        rocking
        shifting

progress measured
in the beats

    of landscape
        changing

we celebrate
    the seasons
eulogize
    potential

      these footsteps
      behind us
           coming louder

           coming clearer

      foot beats waltzing
      with heartbeats trailing
      until
      we close our eyes

      and hear a final tap

      that last note
      of the heart
      and the foot
          echo

              off the edge
                 of sky

from a precipice

i.

i listen to children babble
about the canyons
i've already travelled --

but tonight i confess
that all my memories held
are of eyes closed

come tomorrow
       like today
i will pretend that i know

even when i've
already forgotten the sound
      of hearts
           beating

i watch the lives passing
as faces
become backs
      becoming
           silhouettes

silhouettes slowly
dancing
then fading

this grey
      into black

      and then
           into night

dancing then
fading
behind echoes
    left

those sliding rifts of blues
stolen from a page
of night
and music
where toys
and death
are two notes
    of equal measure
    in even the
        sweetest song

and still
this breath and
this breath still

this breeze
this wind
    whispering

    down all the paths
    as i search
        for roots beneath
            the fallen trees

the forest
is shrinking

ii.

bend the bars
of today and bury
yesterday's picture
       beneath the wing
            of tomorrow

listen to the echo
       of dead hands
            clapping

sit quiet beside water
lapping the rock
       of history's bank
            destiny's shore

watch the leaves
even before their fall
struggle to wear

       the colours
       of the setting sun

we speak but
only in words

as we whisper
       in vision

we then reminded that

voice is forever
       tied to the earth
while passion
       rides the clouds

iii.

i've seen stairs
       climbing stairs
              climbing stairs
                     climbing stairs

and prophets
wander halls
       without ears

walk the wind

ride the wind

listen

catch new words
       coming on edges

catch their first breath
in an echo of
       unspoken word

ride the fine edge of thought

taste the blood
       in its sharpness

as you place it

       to your mouth

       then to your ear

      and then
           to your wrist

stand on the backside
of edges exploding
      in measured and
      constant succession

      leaving each new moment
          as instant

          in the haze
              to stand
                on its own

and then on each side
these crackling pictures
      of burning passion

and echoes of bridges
      crumbling

sit

sit quietly
in search
of the morning
      that never comes

and sleep
      on its stair
           lightly

watch

while tomorrow
rests silent
    between two covers
before us
    as an endless book

    and waits for us
    to swallow
        each page

cancer
for Julio G.

i walk the path
of the tracheotomy
along these fields
    of radiation
        and ghosts

and the sound of my own
voice
    only memory's
    whisper now

still i can hear
that first echo
of its distant rolling
cadenced sound

relentlessly
    spinning
    swirling

        inside
as i sit
alone
    here
and here
my ears yearn
    for any sound
    but this silence

    waltzing
        awkwardly
        clumsily
            endlessly
    with my low rasping
        breath

i am plagued
with this
bandaged mask
of cancer
    where my
    perfect throat
        used to glow

this heir
delivered
    from the womb

    of denial

this heir
born of the
    consummation
    of innocence
        and vanity

once

on the bed of
    immortality
        assumed

prisoner

bars of steel
plated image
behind rolls of
barbed and tangled
thought

freedom's breeze shifts
beyond our grasp
between the mesh
the bars

we stand inside a room
of four cornered
logic

and paint ourselves
into one
      of each

we divide the light
into endless names
then we speak
in the language
      of shadows

wisdom's casket rests
on the floor
open and
before us

the ceiling deceives

      it is not sky

the bars are real
the wire real

that breath
of freedom
      real as well

the corners capture
the paint betrays

the walls imprison
the gate

the gate

this unlocked gate

must surely be
          illusion

weight

and a hundred years
hence

we are but pictures
of bones

skeletons
walking
on carpets
of broken clocks

behind a black
thin veil
and the staccato
of the steel
drums

that processional
march
of the endless
tomorrow

and the promise
then of that parade
of lost sight and
lost sound

lost then
lost
then lost
      again

to skulls
without ears

to skulls with
blank sockets

empty chambers

to blood dripping
from hollow chests

as skin slips

through fingers
without flesh

      to grab
      to hold

      to feel

bones

waiting
for sinew
for warmth
      wanting

as memories fly
in the language
of flesh

flesh
that measure of both
destiny
      and distance

this
that infinite
wait

and

then the weight
of the skin

over eyes

blinded by
      vision

eyes

measuring
universes
in a glance

oblivious still
      to the galaxies
           of atoms

all here
as lost thought wanders

down broken corridors
of life

and then only bones
left dancing

      around hourglasses

        before an orchestra
           of calendars

pages slipping
sand sliding

air
flesh
bones
    grow heavy

earth forever follows
humbling herself

carving caverns for tears
    horizons for laughter

painting skylines without brushes

painting magic without mirrors

calling herself earth
she offers it all
offers herself and
we each
    wait our turn

as we

both a hundred years
    before

and a hundred years
    hence

only bones

skeletons walking
on the broken face
    of tomorrow
with the broken feet
    of today

all beneath
the shadow and
faint ticking of
    yesterday's clock

mirror

chimneys
made of glass

can neither conceal
nor contain

    the fire

    the smoke

glass eyes
watching

glass eyes falling

    knowing

    searching

    remembering

marble faces
sitting on glass
    tables

facing windows

dreaming
of marble chimneys

and wishing they

    were glass

barrio

after Sandra Cisneros' collection "Loose Woman"

jazz musician and
the distant poetry
      from the barrio

and a life
i can but only read

a life i may
      never touch
you said he
called you
      his "amiga"

      his "corazon"
in better times

before he turned
himself
      into air
      and light
in the blackest night
behind the darkest wall

but i stand as you do
on this side still

i here

having touched
the same dark walls
always with but
my own white fingers

still
yet
forever
> skin against wall
> skin against glass
> skin on skin

> walls ever different
> skin always
>> the same

you there

the perfumed ink
dabbed on your neck
> your thigh and
>> then on each page

and beside
> that scent
and with
> each title
> each dream
>> each memory

every page
> waiting
each neck
> stretching
then both
in realization
> turned

even in the distance
the breath shared
eyes looking through
the darkness
    for daylight
    for other eyes
        watching

your stanzas fell
like petals
    stolen in an
        autumn breeze

and barrio's eyes
blink back words
bleed notes in
    silence
    spanish jazz and

a whisper

a tear

a sigh

another leaf
    fallen

a memory
    losing

a wisdom
    calling

and another day
calling back to
those who remain

for time

for perfumed lives

to allow us to feast
to scavenge
these only days
coloured
textured
      in ash

    and leaf

rain

and it was
on a day
      like today

that the first man
watched the clouds
wash the sun
from the sky

and it was
on a day
      like today

that the first river
rolled from a splash
and was born to the
parents of gravity
and rock

and it was
on a day
      like today

that the darkness
washed and fell
like boulders
and the first
thunder roared

and it was
on a day
      like today

that the water
surged and washed
away every road
and every bridge
from my house
       to yours

tribute

i.

there was an instant
before there was
    anything

yet there was
everything
    waiting

air waiting
    for breath
darkness waiting
    for colour

as bits of rock
    and dust
raced and
    rolled
    and turned
over themselves
    waiting for earth

and shards of sound
    soft low
    shrill harsh
scrambled and tumbled
    waiting for words

as single
> instants
> seconds

were waiting
> in tandem

to be plucked
> randomly

out of the air
from this trail
> this glistening
> translucent spear

of iridescent green light
flowing
intersected in
> every direction
> every dimension
> by infinite numbers
> of rays of similar light
> each and all passing
> through each second
>> waiting   and

those were

these are

the maps
> of destiny

ii.

within interwoven trails

of iridescent light
earth and sound and
the panorama of the sky

horizon stood

needing only itself
beauty inherent
      absolute

but soon eyes followed

and mathematicians
looked into
the dirt
the air
the water
and saw numbers
      watching other numbers

astronomers
looked up
into the shadow
and saw candescent
embers of light and
      flashes of motion

and dancers
beneath their feet
felt the motion
the rhythm

the sway
the pull and
      the spin of the earth

and writers
      saw words forming
as the poets
      saw the spaces between

and the children
saw it all
with a voice inside
      but would never tell…

iii.

in this world of eyes

image buries essence
as fingers slide
       on top

surfaces mask
hold beneath
    lines
      volume
          edges

edges

sun kissing shadow

warmth in layers
      passing through

ears hearing
    the thought of
    every ear

ecstasy wearing
    tragedy's echo

lifeblood flowing

within us and

       between us

iv.

and the great poets

would tell you in depth
about all these things

but i cannot

as i try

i attempt to immortalize
the moments as i hold them
softly clenched

their cold dry surface
against colder drier palm

but the great poets
feel the breeze
of each second passing
flowing into and half-around
       their fingers
       open palm

and as if untouched
these wisps of air
       swirl their hands

with lines slowing

edges sharpening
generating
       fine iridescent rays
       of original light and

as their fingers fold and
then ever so slowly open again

to drop bits of rock and dust

      into buckets of sound

            and canyons of voice

passage
for Morgan K.
– from an obituary, child born/died the same day

you, who was not allowed
to taste
    either the sweetness
    or the bitterness
        of this life

as but for an instant
    your eyes graced
    the light of this
        morning

were the colours
    not quite so vivid
    as you'd hoped
        that they might be

was the air not
quite as sweet
    as your mother
    had promised
        in your sleep

did the darkness
    frighten
was the light
    so blinding
was the noise
    too deafening

was it all
    overwhelming

or did you not wait
long enough
    to find a rainbow
        inside the haze

not wait for the scent
    of the springtime
        to fill your mouth
        and then your lungs

not wait to wear
that warm, sweet
    blanket of twilight
    between those worlds
        of darkness and light

or not wait to hear
that single chord
    of softness in
    your mother's voice
        calling

        calling…

            calling…

or did you simply choose
instead

to go from a world
without voice
without language
> with which to describe
> the lines and threads
> of pain and beauty

> through an instant
> of each

and into another world
that other world
that has neither reason
nor ambition
to define
> the boundaries
>> of either

shadows

fear settles rests
behind the eyes
of courage

as it hides within
the camouflage
of what it could
      never be
still fully standing yet
at the mirror of
what it
      truly is

the endless facade

what should stand
by itself alone quietly
falls into its shadow

what should live
eternal ever so
slowly dies at dawn

how many night shades
of violet burgundy purple
have passed unnoticed
or forgotten since

as evening gave up
her will
her spirit
her colour
and threw herself
      then into the darkness

and cast her desire
into the depths
     of a bottomless pit

left now as only haze
     around the moon

these remains of passion

these remnants of haze
that linger

memory's tears

this reminder of hours spent
focused on the distance

those times of landmarks
placed upon the years

those times
those countless times
of giving up the passion
and the colours
of the night

and now
a thousand stone walls
approaching

and i no longer allowed

to change
or climb

i am left
with but regret
instead

as my bones now
too weak
too old
too brittle here
to stand

and, yes, i know
i will never
have to fight
        another war

but i shall never

        dance

language

i watched time
as it watched the faces
of clocks lose sight
    of their shadows

and saw from all things
their threads
flowing backward
through the moving
    breath of time

these oblivious threads
continually and
innocently flowing

always leaving but still
forever never questioning
how strongly tied

yet by the source
how loosely guided
and left unattended

threads crossing
woven into blankets

then woven again
into pieces of time

and i'm walking

i'm sitting

i've already written
this poem
a hundred times
right here
      before

and all the faces

all the breath
sounds the same
smells the same
      bleeds the same

this hunted trail of words
leaves its tracks
in the dirt
in faded light
and splintered time

we watch
we sit
we listen
to their breath
      in the shadow
but never see their eyes

the ancients had a single word
a single answer
to all the questions of life

but they buried
that word in the earth
in the grave that they dug
and dug with the same tool
even their elders used
to excavate both water
and resurrect the first wheel

father
father of this dirt

this dirt wearing
the imprint of my soul

your answer blows
and burns my eyes
fills my ears
fills my pockets
fills my shoes

waits to fill my heart

in dust to dust

dust waits
    for dust

earth waits
    for eyes

blood thicker than

    still mixes in
    crimson tears

as behind shallow
graves we dig
each
with our own
pointed spade

this search for truth

and each shovelful
brings up only more dirt

mixed
with whispers
    of chains
in the language
    of wheels

destiny

i am a potter

i was born a potter
my father before me
was a potter
as was his father
before him

it is my heritage

it becomes my destiny

>to make bowls
>for a world that has
>no soup

reading

i sat
spellbound

lost in a blizzard
of words
blinding
words on
      words on
           words drifting

thought on thought
sifting to
that space between

this wind of words
frigid
biting

but voice

voice
sweet voice
sweeter chorus
metaphoric rhapsody

innocent chords
hiding melancholy notes
      like night and water
      both hide the tide

i was lost
motionless
in timeless gap

bathed ambiguous
in partial light
in colour vague

a twilight red
escaping horizon
skims my flesh
breaks within

red horizon
coursing now

flowing exploding
through my veins
my heart and

as she whispered
the words in and out
back out and then in

those words she freed
from her lungs and mouth

spilled from her spirit
fell from her lips and
filled the room
in fragrance so sweet
      that it rose to the ceiling

then dripped from the rafters
in droplets
of warm honey
      and tears

my ears bled
for the pain
that she carried
and my eyes caught
the evening flow out
from her soul

her spirit exhaled
the room fell within

her words
with the wings
of raven

flew into the twilight
and back through
      the night

hung in the air
like a snowflake
      in autumn

then turned into angels
as her voice
      cleared the sky

and that night
her words like a river

runs slowly and
then hides like tomorrow
just beyond
      the next ridge

that reading

that evening
of music on song

hung
like a teardrop
on the edge of extinction

my heart grew eyes

      in order to weep

today

i am
only this
        single instant

and this instant
        yesterday's challenge
        tomorrow's mist

how thin
        this trail
how lucid
        this colour
how cleansing
        this light

i am
silence

i am
the seed
        of tomorrow

i am
the wind
        set still

i am
morning
        without light

i am
evening
colour

i am
the final
chapter of
an untold story

i am
a single
note in
nine hundred thousand chords

and still
i am but
yesterday's
    breath

and tomorrow's
    vapour

seed

"bring it in the morning

the moon is right" he said

he chose the earth

he tilled until
the soil sat warm
and moist

he prepared the bed
and taking these new
whispers of things
held in his hand
he slowly sowed them

       straight and
       deep

"he had a way with seed"
       they said

he had a way
       with words

now both
planted

       it was spring

shade and shadow

in the shadow
of a mountain cliff
wrestling with her shadow
a young girl
grasping
reaching
died alone

and as she fell

no one heard
      her final thoughts
      her final whimper

here
now
on this edge
      of that cliff

in this newer
shade
i hear both
      those echoes

      still

legends

remove yourself
far enough
until the jagged edge
becomes
first the line

then the balance

discover

sense under your feet
the spin of the world

feel the seasons' breeze
through your hair
trading green forests
for golden aspen
becoming white and icy
background calling
back the green again

who left me with no questions
as i stand in a field of answers

here in the shadow
of legacies
as i plant my soul
in the imprint of where
their feet have been

those pathways
never chosen
the answers slowly wilting

here upon and beside
passageways left untrodden
trails left unattended
both draped in web
and calcified frost

but still here
and here still
these memories

those memories of

even in this billowing
smoke and soot
a thousand lifetimes
could not have prepared me
for the beauty i saw
the first time
i opened my eyes

death

the words left me
empty

the news
of your death

the funeral

no comfort
in the eulogy
      eloquent

no sound
could have covered
the hushed silence
and the resounding
echo of that
final breath
      spent

here in this stead
the wonder
waste

the wake

a sterile dressing
bandage
      of family
      friends

a tourniquet
        to a mortal wound

words
        forced
                floating

smiles carried
      on the wings
      of tears

these images

of you into
the darkness
vanishing
fading
      beneath
      timeless cloud
      shadowed loss

visions

a thousand times
revisited

i see you dying

i watch you die
        again

        again

        again and

even in this new air
the scent lingers

that fragrance
        so sweet
        so moist
of birthing
        and sweat

as you are and were
silently delivered
from this world

        to the next

spirit

glaze
frozen still
on the edge

morning's
horizon

what to make of
this transparency
in the wake
      of an always
      tomorrow
this

this shadow
at the helm of
      yesterday's fog

this twilight

veneer
coloured brown haze
against
that slight sienna floor

this new day conceived

in the distance
barely visible
almost indiscernible

a silhouette

a single figure left
standing

a solitary being

    woman?
    man?
    mother?
    god?
    mistress?
    brother?
    maid?

this solitary being
with broom in hand
stooped and standing

on the edge
    of the sunrise and

slowly
deliberately
sweeping away
    the broken pieces

        of yesterday

void

time
    invisible highway

thread
    elusive
passage
    quiet
    blind

from this thought
to another

today into sunset

from this world
to the next

pavement

rocky
rutted
vacant
    journey

and i

travel
blindly
never knowing
    tomorrow

tell me
again
    of the caress
    of the dew
        on this blade
        of grass

        for i
        may never feel

sing
of the song
    inherent
    that instant love

        the mother feels
        for her new-born
        child

        for i
        may never know

tell me
    again
of the first
    passage
    to india
and of the
    second passage
    back

then tell me
how much
    time
it takes
the space to fill

    a thought

    a thimble

    a trembling heart

solitude

solitude
took the brush
from my fingers

and painted
the colour
of its night
    on the back
    of my hand

and i could smell
her breath
    of roses
and could taste
the blood
    on her thorn

and there was
a passionate fire
in her eyes
    neither anger
    nor lust

and she told me
of a time when
there was
    no poetry

    nothing symbolic
    no canvas
    or brush
        or back
        of a wrist

and a time when
all things carried
but their own face

and of a time
of everything
      walking backward
           and with all their
                eyes closed

Author's Biographical Note:

Bruce Kauffman lives in Kingston, Ontario and is a poet, writer and editor. A chapbook of his poetry, *seed*, (The Plowman), was published in 2005, and with consideration to be re-published and bound by Hidden Brook Press. A stand-alone poem, "streets" (Thee Hellbox Press) was published in 2009. *The Texture of Days, In Leaf and Ash* (Hidden Brook Press) is his first full collection of poetry.

His work has appeared in numerous periodicals and anthologies, including a book review in *The Antigonish Review* (fall /2010) for John Pigeau's *The Nothing Waltz* (Hidden Brook Press). His poetry has also appeared in two plays, *The Garbage and the Flowers* (2008) and *A Moveable Feast* (2009). His poem "potter", appearing in this collection, was shortlisted in the 1995 Poiesis Poetry Competition.

In 1997/1998 he was research editor and volunteer coordinator for a poetry short collection and reference manual, the *Poiesis Poetry Guide* (1998). Beginning in 2011 he coordinated and edited *That Not Forgotten* (Hidden Brook Press), a 400 page poetry/short fiction anthology of 118 locally tied poets and authors, launched in September 2012.

In May 2010, he began hosting a weekly spoken word radio show on CFRC 101.9fm (Queen's University, Kingston, ON) called "finding a voice" and now also hosts a blogspace for that show at: findingavoiceoncfrcfm.wordpress.com

As well, he hosts a monthly open mic reading series called "poetry @ the artel" (launched in May, 2009), and in June of 2012 began a quarterly series of "stream of consciousness" writing workshops (Kingston based, but will be spreading in 2013 to outlying areas).

He is a member of a local writers group. He joined the Wintergreen Studios Press Advisory Board as Acquisitions Editor. He is a member of the CCLA (Canada Cuba Literary Alliance) and is one of the Canadian Editors of CCLA's literary journal, *The Ambassador*. He is currently editing other works and working on two of his own manuscripts.

Contact: bruce.kauffman@hotmail.com
         bruce.kauffman99@gmail.com

Photographer's Biographical Note:

Eleanor Leonne Bennett is a 16 year old internationally award winning photographer and artist who has won first place honours with National Geographic, The World Photography Organisation, Nature's Best Photography, Papworth Trust, Mencap, and The Woodland Trust and Postal Heritage. Her photography has been published in the Telegraph, The Guardian, BBC News Website and on the cover of books and magazines in both the United States and Canada. Her art is globally exhibited, having shown work in London, Paris, Indonesia, Los Angeles, Florida, Washington, Scotland, Wales, Ireland, Canada, Spain, Germany, Japan, Australia and at The Environmental Photographer of the year Exhibition (2011), as well as many other locations.

She was also the only person from the UK to have her work displayed in the National Geographic and Airbus run See The Bigger Picture global exhibition tour with the United Nations International Year Of Biodiversity 2010.

www.eleanorleonnebennett.zenfolio.com

The cover:

Eleanor says:

Feather and Bone 2 is a mixed media construction of file and linoleum, chicken bones and a peacock feather. It is one of my favourites.

I love to use some aspect of fire in my work. I feel connected to all-consuming flames and the rebirth of textures that exist on the other side.

Books in the North Shore Series

Find full information at
– http://www.HiddenBrookPress.com/b-NShore.html

Anthologies

Changing Ways is a book of prose by Cobourg area authors including: Jean Edgar Benitz, Patricia Calder, Fran O'Hara Campbell, Leonard D'Agostino, Shane Joseph, Brian Mullally. Editor: Jacob Hogeterp – Prose – ISBN – 978-1-897475-22-5

That Not Forgotten - Editor – Bruce Kauffman with 118 authors – Prose and Poetry – ISBN – 978-1-897475-89-8

First set of five books

— **M.E. Csamer** – Kingston – *A Month Without Snow*
  – Prose – ISBN – 978-1-897475-87-2
— **Elizabeth Greene** – Kingston – *The Iron Shoes*
  – Poetry – ISBN – 978-1-897475-76-6
— **Richard Grove** – Brighton – *A Family Reunion*
  – Prose – ISBN – 978-1-897475-90-2
— **R.D. Roy** – Trenton – *A Pre emptive Kindness*
  – Prose – ISBN – 978-1-897475-80-3
— **Eric Winter** – Cobourg – *The Man In The Hat*
  – Poetry – ISBN – 978-1-897475-77-3

Second set of five books

— **Janet Richards** – Belleville – *Glass Skin*
  – Poetry – ISBN – 978-1-897475-01-0
— **R.D. Roy** – Trenton – *Three Cities*
  – Poetry – ISBN – 978-1-897475-96-4
— **Wayne Schlepp** – Cobourg – *The Darker Edges of the Sky*
  – Poetry – ISBN – 978-1-897475-99-5
— **Benjamin Sheedy** – Kingston – *A Centre in Which They Breed*
  – Poetry – ISBN – 978-1-897475-98-8
— **Patricia Stone** – Peterborough – *All Things Considered*
  – Prose – ISBN – 978-1-897475-04-1

Third set of five books

— **Mark Clement** – Cobourg – *Island In the Shadow*
   – Poetry – ISBN – 978-1-897475-08-9
— **Anthony Donnelly** – Brighton – *Fishbowl Fridays*
   – Prose – ISBN – 978-1-897475-02-7
— **Chris Faiers** – Marmora – *ZenRiver Poems & Haibun*
   – Poetry – ISBN – 978-1-897475-25-6
— **Shane Joseph** – Cobourg – *Fringe Dwellers* Second Edition
   – Prose – ISBN – 978-1-897475-44-7
— **Deborah Panko** – Cobourg – *Somewhat Elsewhere*
   – Poetry – ISBN – 978-1-897475-13-3

Forth set of five books

— **Diane Dawber** – Bath – *Driving, Braking and Getting out to Walk*
   – Poetry – ISBN – 978-1-897475-40-9
— **Patrick Gray** – Port Hope – *This Grace of Light*
   – Poetry – ISBN – 978-1-897475-34-8
— **John Pigeau** – Kingston – *The Nothing Waltz*
   – Prose – ISBN – 978-1-897475-37-9
— **Mike Johnston** – Cobourg – *Reflections Around the Sun*
   – Poetry – ISBN – 978-1-897475-38-6
— **Kathryn MacDonald** – Shannonville – *Calla & Édourd*
   – Prose – ISBN – 978-1-897475-39-3

Fifth set of three books

— **Tara Kainer** – Kingston – *When I Think On Your Lives*
   – Poetry– ISBN – 978-1-897475-68-3
— **Morgan Wade** – Kingston – *The Last Stoic*
   – Novel – ISBN – 978-1-897475-63-8
— **Kathryn MacDonald** – Shannonville – *A Breeze You Whisper*
   – Poetry – ISBN – 978-1-897475-66-9

Sixth set of three books

—**Bruce Kauffman** – *The Texture of Days, in Ash and Leaf*
   – Poetry – ISBN - 978-1-897475-86-7
— **Chris Faiers** – *Eel Pie Island Dharma: A hippie memoir/haibun*
   – A memoir in haibun form – ISBN - 978-1-897475-92-8
— **Theodore Michael Christou** – *an overbearing eye*
   – Poetry – ISBN – 978-1-897475-93-5

www.ingramcontent.com/pod-product-compliance
Lightning Source LLC
Chambersburg PA
CBHW021110080526
44587CB00010B/469